5-7-5

Toni Williams

Presentation by *BookLeaf Publishing*

Web: www.bookleafpub.com

E-mail: info@bookleafpub.com

ISBN: 9789358315882

First edition 2023

This is dedicated to 7 year old Toni Jean- don't give up.

ACKNOWLEDGEMENT

I would like to acknowledge my friends and family who love and support me through all the seasons of life.

Volume

Anger consumes us
Rancid energy fills air
Exhausting my soul

Heart races madly
Anxiety on full blast
Mind scattered loosely

Silent wishes blare
Echos of love lost madly
Deafening unrest

Narcissist v empath
Unequivocal death match
Champion loses

Jellyfishin'

Was not my best self
Tomorrow brings a new day
Forgive- forget- pray

Needing that hard pause
To get me from A to B
Where my mind is still

Synapses are broke
Overwhelmed by all the sounds
Chaos is my life

Adhd is
My superpower and fault
Riddling my life

No navigation
For the fast roaring waters
Sink or swim -I'll float

Shine

Joyous bright laughter
Fills my space with vivid light
Kaleidoscope eyes

Tiny feet and hands
Making imprints on my heart
Smudging my focus

Days with no end near
Years pass in two blinks
Long lost childhood

Let me love you now
Like I have never been loved
Share your light with me

Hold my hand today
Pick flowers in the meadow
Carelessly being

You are my happy
You are my truth and my gift
Bittersweet regalo

Mutualism perks
Between mother and her brood
Exist naturally

Submerge

Another shit storm
Caught without the proper sails
Waves engulf my ship

Drowning violently
Praying to my creator
Silence takes over

Ruby

Your voice came to me
Echoed from the stars above
Starfire is born

Self-destruct

Nerves frazzled - get away
Let me stew in my silence
Effortless loathing

Jasper

Visions of Pele
Volcano eruption blast
Goddess of my heart

Azul

Blue like curaçao
Blessings from Henry Rollins
Paradise lost dream

Vision

Heaven is white
Billowy and inviting
Beneath the sea

Maple

Intuition spark
10/10/2020 chance
Greetings from fortune

Jesus

12

Hand on my shoulder
Came to me one night in prayer
Heart activated

Feast

Instant karma, please
Served on a silver platter
No garnish needed

Indio

Ferris Wheel romance
Coachella night adventures
Truly the fungi

Ruminate

15

Thoughts that never stop
Daydreams that continue at night
Constantly aloof

Repent

Always quick to judge
Criticize, mock, jeer and point
Your day is coming

Toni Jean

17

Deep inside of me
Resides a broken little girl
Yearning for a hug

Maximo

Strong little lion
My Leo prince roars loudly
powerful presence

Scarlet

Innate gifts within
Wizardly like ol' Merlin
Reincarnated

Earth

Buried my son today
Said goodbye and wished him well
Two faint lines appeared

Halloween

Hunters moon shines full
Ghosts goblins ghouls and warlocks
Feast with me and mine

Being

Mother-Daughter-Wife
Sacred duties to fulfill
Constant state of Stone